CONV
RECIPE
BOOK

ACN 009550841

This edition published 2015

ISBN 0 949089 10 9

Photographs courtesy of the Allport Library and Museum of Fine Arts, The Tasmanian Archives and the Apple Industry Museum, Grove, Huonville.

Above: Arriving at Port Arthur in 1840.
Below: A cruise ship and visitors in yachts arrive in 1995.

Above: The Port Arthur Jetty.
Left: The armoury & powder store.
Below: The hospital & asylum.

CONTENTS

Soups

Fish

Sauces

Vegetables

Meat

Puddings

Sandwiches

Cakes, Slices & Biscuits

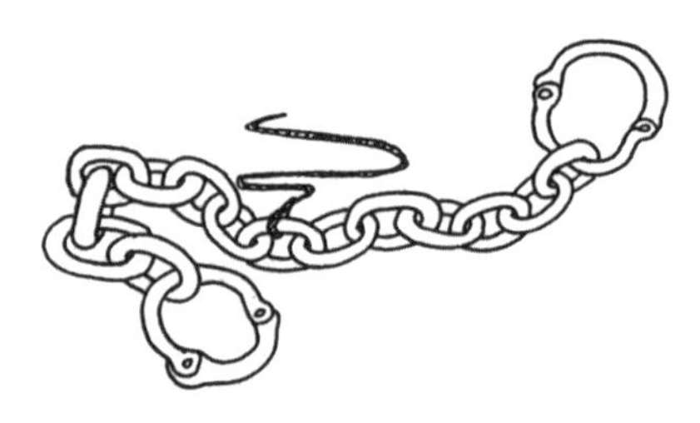

A BIOGRAPHY - <u>BALDWIN,</u> Bessie Florence

When Bessie Baldwin came to London in 1837 she was 19. Nothing is known about her parents or early childhood, but it is known she came from Kent, so it is probable that she was born and raised on a farm. England in the 1820s was a country of contrasts with the birth of the industrial revolution in a depressed society of massive unemployment following the end of the Napoleonic Wars. Although Napoleon had called the English "a nation of shopkeepers," a middle class was virtually non-existent. There were only two classes, the very rich and the very poor.

Bessie Baldwin, because of her farm upbringing, was fortunate enough to find employment with pastrycook and baker, Thos. Edenwell, who, it seems, had his bakery hard by the House of Commons in Westminster, and was a self-styled "Pastrycook to the Honourable Members." In October 1839, Bessie Baldwin was charged in the Old Bailey with "riotous behaviour." According to the evidence it would seem that she was one of the early womens' liberationists. She had demanded a pay rise of one penny a week from her employer to bring her wages up to five pence a week. Edenwell, who seems to have been a cheapskate of considerable note, refused this modest request. Bessie Baldwin set about wrecking his shop including, to quote from the evidence, "assaulting the said Thos. Edenwell by striking him with a rabbit pie, and then beating him about the head with the pie dish." For this little escapade, she was sentenced to transportation to the Colony of Van Dieman's Land for seven years.

On December 14th, 1839, she was embarked with 182 other women and 24 children on the 427 ton barque 'Gilbert Henderson' under Captain J. Tweedie. When the 'Gilbert Henderson' arrived in Hobart on April 24th, 1840, Bessie Baldwin was immediately removed to the Female Factory, a house of correction for females at the Cascades, Degrave Street, in South Hobart.

What happened on the voyage is hearsay, and comes from Captain Tweedie himself, thus supplying the Colony with a juicy bit of scandal to be whispered around.

It appears that the Surgeon Superintendent on the voyage, in charge of all convicts, was Sir John Hamett. According to Captain Tweedie, Sir John was a notorious rakehell who squandered his not inconsiderable personal fortune gambling and wenching in London. Again according to the good Captain, Sir John had taken the post of Surgeon in the ship because of a scandal involving the wife of a high official of the Court, which could have resulted in Sir John being publicly horsewhipped. It would seem that Sir John's notoriety did not end once the barque had left England's shores. It was not long before he had picked the most comely of the women under his charge for his personal pleasures. When Captain Tweedie tried to intervene, Sir John called him a "d...d meddling rogue" and reminded him that he was there to "steer your d...d boat and mind your place!" As Sir John had friends in high places, Captain Tweedie did not press the matter, but he noted his protests in the ship's log.

In his cups (which was often) Sir John had boasted that his most sterling attribute was a good eye for women and horseflesh, which was probably why his eye lighted on Bessie Baldwin early in the voyage. However, in this case, he had taken on rather more than he could handle. His persistent advances were continually rebuffed which, according to Captain Tweedie, inflamed him all the more. On the 28th day out, Sir John ordered the girl to his cabin at night. What happened was not witnessed, save that the watch heard an uproar in the surgeon's flat, and then Sir John staggered on deck bleeding from a massive cut extending from his right eye to the crown of his head. Bessie Baldwin followed, candlestick in hand, and she had to be forcibly restrained from beating Sir John's head to a pulp. Streaming blood, Sir John was escorted back to his cabin, and Bessie Baldwin was taken to the brig where she spent the remainder of the voyage.

It is astonishing that Sir John did not take punitive action against the girl, either sentencing her to be flogged or, at least, a drop over the side in the ducking box. Suffice it to say that Sir John spent almost the rest of the voyage in his cabin, and left the ship for Government House in Hobarton sporting a half healed scar nearly five inches long.

Bessie Baldwin was not assigned immediately, which was the usual course, but sent direct to the female house of correction. According to Captain Tweedie, she had been unjustly treated and deserved a medal rather than punishment. The female factory of that period was indeed a house of correction, the inmates being those considered unemployable and hard cases. The main occupation was picking oakum.

From the few records available it would seem that Bessie Baldwin carried on her good work as a womens' liberationist by continually demanding better working conditions and urging the inmates to riot... it was said she was a ringleader in. the famous escapade which was a pointed insult to a visiting Vice-Regal party. Sir John Franklin, Lady Franklin (a noted 'do-gooder'), and a clergyman, the Reverend Bedford of whom it was said he paid more attention to the bottle than the bible, were the party concerned. The ladies showed their displeasure at the visit by hiking up their skirts and showing their bare backsides, which they simultaneously smacked with their hands, making a loud musical noise. This was the work of a moment, and although constables and warders were there in plenty, yet 300 women could not well be all arrested and tried for such an offence! It was said of Sir John that "he turned away and blushed". How Lady Franklin and Rev. Bedford reacted, is not known.

In 1842 fate was to take a hand in the life of Bessie Baldwin. It came about due to the fact that Sir John liked to assign the females himself. He needed an assistant cook and pastrycook at Government House, and after an exhaustive search among the female convicts he finally had a short list which included Bessie Florence Baldwin. Life in the dreary female factory had chastened her by this time. The sheer monotony and harsh discipline had finally cut into her soul. After all, who wanted a woman with the temper of a vixen and who was likely to wield a pie dish or candlestick with unerring aim? Finally, a slightly desperate Sir John employed her at Government House, where, according to the records, she became "a model of obedient womanly virtue".

Such was her virtue in the culinary field that before Sir John relinquished his post in the Colony, he granted her a pardon. Now comes the mystery. Bessie Baldwin never married in the Colony, and all that is known is that she left Tasmania in 1849 for New South Wales, and nothing was heard of her then or since.

What still remain are her recipes. These were recorded by a Governess to a landed family, and they have come down as some of the finest Colonial recipes ever.

****

CONVERSION

Ounces to grams (approximate)

Oz.	Gr.	Oz.	Gr.
1	28	9	255
2	57	10	283
3	85	11	312
4	113	12	340
5	141	13	368
6	170	14	397
7	198	15	426
8	227	16	454

Millilitres

1 Tablespoon - 25 ml
1 Dessertspoon - 12.5 ml
1 Teaspoon - 5 ml
1 Cup - 228 ml
3/4 Cup - 170 ml
1/2 Cup - 114 ml
1/4 Cup - 57 ml

Fluid Ounces to Millilitres

Fl.Oz.	ml	Fl.Oz.	ml
1	28	11	312
2	57	12	341
3	85	13	369
4	114	14	398
5	142	15	426
6	170	16	454
7	199	17	483
8	228	18	511
9	256	19	540
10	284	20	568

Oven Tempratures

Degrees

F	C
275	140
300	150
325	160
350	180
375	190
400	200
425	220
450	230

CAKE TINS

6 inch - 15cm
7 inch - 18cm
9 inch - 23cm

Loaf Tin: 9" x 5" - 23 x 12cm
Bar Tin: 10" x 3" - 25 x 8cm
Lamington: 11" x 7" - 28 x 18cm

In recipes from colonial times, some of the ingredients listed are not widely used nowadays, and are replaced by other products. For example, fat and dripping are often replaced with cooking oil, and self raising flour was not known.

SOUPS

BROWN SOUP

Small shin of beef, cut in large pieces. Put a little dripping or the marrow from bones into a large saucepan. Dredge meat with flour, and brown well. Add 3 quarts of water, bring to boil, and simmer for 5 hours. Strain, leave till next day. Put a little dripping in saucepan, and fry 1 onion, 1 turnip, 2 carrots, cut in dice. Take fat from soup, put into saucepan with the vegetables, and simmer for 1-1/2 hours. Add salt and pepper to taste. Serve with toasted sippets.

CHOWDER

Cut up one onion, and simmer in butter till golden brown, then add a cup of water and a cup of sliced potatoes. Simmer until potatoes are soft, then add three or four unsweetened biscuits, a pint of milk, little pepper and salt. Simmer a few minutes, then add oysters (fresh or bottled). Do not let it boil after oysters are added.

OX-TAIL SOUP

1 ox-tail
1 oz butter
2 turnips
1 head of celery
3 quarts water
1 slice of ham
2 carrots
3 onions
pepper & salt

Skim well, and simmer very gently for 4 hours, or until the tails are tender. Take them out. Skim and strain the soup, thicken with flour. Put back the tails. Simmer for 5 minutes and serve.

A packet of mushroom soup used as thickening for gravies in which meat is to be simmered, adds a rich and delicious flavour.

LENTIL SOUP

8 ozs lentils
3 onions
2lb parsnips
1 oz brown sugar
pepper & salt
1 carrot. chopped
1 leek
3 large crusts of bread
parsley

Wash and pick the lentils, soak overnight. Boil with the vegetables and bread for 3 hours, pass the whole through a colander, heat again, and serve. Costs little, and will last two or three days.

TOMATO SOUP

2 lb tomatoes
1/2 pint milk
butter. pepper. salt to taste
1/2 teaspoon carb soda

Cut tomatoes in 4, cover with boiling water till soft. Add carb soda. Boil about 10 minutes, strain, pour back in saucepan, add milk. When boiling, thicken with flour. Add about 1 dessertspoon of butter, pepper and salt.

POTATO SOUP

2lb or 3lb potatoes, boiled soft, with 1 small onion, 1 turnip (1 carrot or parsnip if liked), 1 quart of good stock and cream or milk to taste.

PEA SOUP

1 quart split peas
1 slice bacon
2 large carrots
2 turnips
1 head celery
2 quarts water
2lb shin beef
trimmings of rneat or poultry
5 large onions
seasoning to taste
2 quarts of stock or liquor in which a joint of rneat has been boiled.

Boil 4 hours. Strain before using.

RABBIT SOUP

2 rabbits, boil till meat falls from bones. Strain, add diced carrot, turnip and onion, and boil again. Season well with pepper and salt.

SCOTCH BROTH

6lb neck of mutton
5 carrots
2 onions
a little salt
3 quarts water
5 turnips
4 tablespoons barley

As soon as it boils, skim well and simmer for 1-1/2 hours. Before serving add 1 pint milk, a little chopped parsley, and thicken with a little flour.

VEGETABLE SOUP

9 pints water
4 onions
3 or 4 tomatoes
1 cup split peas
4 large carrots
1 head celery
1 cup lentils
pepper & salt

Bring to boil, simmer for 6 hours, and strain.

OYSTER SOUP

Two quarts of oysters
Two tablespoons butter
Pepper and salt
1 quart of milk
1 teacupful hot water

Strain all the liquor from the oysters. Add the water and heat; then add the rest of the ingredients. Cook about 5 minutes. Serve very hot.

CELERY SOUP

Four heads of celery
A little sugar & nutmeg
1/2 pint milk
1/2 teaspoon salt
1/2 pint strong stock
1 quart boiling water

Boil till tender, cast through seive, add stock, and simmer for half an hour.

MULLIGATAWNY SOUP

3 quarts white stock
2 oz butter
juice of 1/2 lemon
2 apples
1 minced onion
2 tablespoons curry powder
2 oz flour
chutney

Fry apples, chutney, curry, onion, in butter for 20 minutes; gradually add flour. Add stock, and boil for 1/2 hour; strain and serve with boiled rice.

WHITE SOUP

Boil a veal bone for 3 hours, with celery, onion, turnip, carrot, and whatever things you may wish that will not make the soup dark. Strain it and boil again. Just before serving it add a pint of cream or milk.

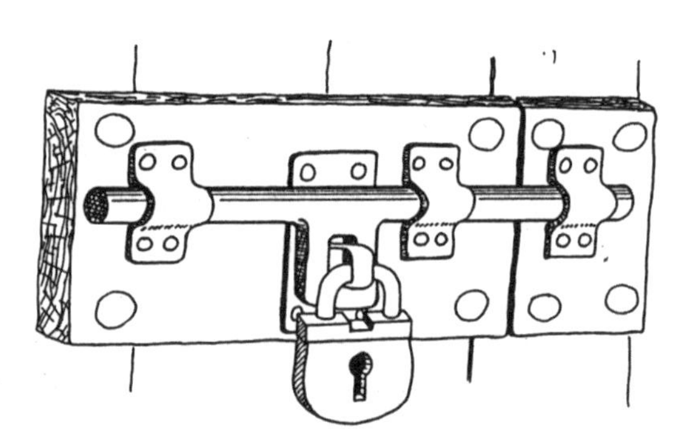

FISH

ANGELS ON HORSEBACK

Pieces of nicely trimmed toast, cut cooked ham or bacon same size, but very thin, lay on toast; then put several oysters on the top; pepper, then pour oyster liquor over the whole. Put in oven till well heated through.

BAKED FISH

Choose a nice large fish, such as a perch or trumpeter; wrap well in buttered paper; place in baking dish; cook in a hot oven for 20 minutes. Remove paper. Pour over fish a prepared white sauce; garnish with parsley and egg.

FISH CREAM

Make an open wall of potatoes on a dish; put in centre a tablespoon of white sauce; cover with pulled fish or salmon sprinkled with pepper and salt, and a few breadcrumbs; cover again with the sauce; then fish, etc. until dish is full. Heat in oven until brown.

SCALLOPED CRAYFISH

Two ounces of butter melted in a stewpan; add flour until thick; then a teacup of milk and two teaspoons of cream. Stir well and let it just boil. Add the crayfish finely cut up with plenty of pepper and salt, and a little cayenne. Do not let it boil any more. Put it into a pied dish, sprinkle with breadcrumbs, and bake 20 minutes.

FISH HASH

One cupful cooked fish
2 cups mashed potatoes
pepper to taste
1 tablespoon melted butter
2 tablespoons cream
1 egg

Heat the fish and potatoes (which may be cooked the day before); add the egg, butter, and cream. Beat until very light, and brown slightly in a frying pan. Fold like an omelette, and serve on a heated dish. This is a nice breakfast dish.

LITTLE PIGS IN BLANKETS

Take large oysters (tinned or fresh), wrap them up in very thin slices of bacon; fry very lightly. Serve on hot toast.

OYSTER FRITTERS

Make a batter as for fritters; chop up oysters, and place in batter. Fry a tablespoon at a time in boiling fat. Serve very hot.

SALMON MOULD

Soak 1/2 oz gelatine in a little water. When soaked dissolve with a little boiling water, add one tin of salmon, pepper and salt to taste. Put together in a saucepan; heat thoroughly. Have ready a hard-boiled egg, chopped and parsley, also chopped. Put parsley and egg in bottom of mould; then add the other ingredients. Let stand till cold.

When frying fish, sprinkle a little salt in the pan before cooking so that the fish will not stick.

If eggs are placed in cold water 2 hours before using, they will beat easier and make cakes lighter.

SALMON CROQUETTES

1 tin salmon
salt to taste
1 tablespoon vinegar
cayenne pepper
1 tablespoon butter
1 egg

Put salmon and other ingredients into a bowl, and mix well, then roll up into small oval shapes and dip in egg and breadcrumbs. Fry a nice brown, then drain on paper, and serve very hot.

SALMON CUTLETS

Dissolve in a saucepan 1 tablespoon of butter; stir in 1 tablespoon flour; add 1/2 cup of milk or water, and boil; then add salmon with the bones taken out. Add pepper, salt, nutmeg, and lemon juice. Take a teaspoon of the mixture, and drop into pepper, salt flour; then into egg and breadcrumbs. Form into shape of cutlets and fry.

To store unbeaten egg yolks, cover with water and leave in fridge. Drain off water before using.

SAUCES

APPLE SAUCE

6 good sized apples
nob of butter size of walnut
sugar to taste

Place in saucepan with enough water to moisten. Boil to a pulp and beat with sugar and butter.

JAM SAUCE

Boil pint of water with 3 oz sugar until reduced to half. Add two tablespoons blackcurrant jam, or any other, juice of 1/2 lemon, and a few drops cochineal. Thicken with 1/2 teaspoon arrowroot. Strain and serve hot over any light coloured pudding.

A mangle with wooden rollers, galvanised bath tubs , and a kitchen furnished with everyday items from the past

Early road transport. Passengers walked up the steeper sections of hills, and the photographer has used a pause while the last passengers catch up.

LEMON SAUCE

Put the grated rind of one lemon and one cup of cold water into saucepan, bring to boil, add juice of lemon, strained. Thicken with cornflour mixed with cold water, and boil a minute or two. Sweeten to taste.

MINT SAUCE

One tablespoon finely chopped mint, 1 dessertspoon sugar or more, dissolved in 3 tablespoons hot water, 3 tablespoons vinegar.

OYSTER SAUCE

Melt 1-1/2oz: butter, add 1/2oz: flour. Add next the liquor of oysters and 1/2 pint milk, half and half of each. Add juice of a lemon, pepper and salt. Add oysters, and just bring to boil.

TOMATO SAUCE FOR ROASTS

6 large tomatoes
1 dessertspoon sugar
1/2 cup breadcrumbs
1 onion, minced
pepper & salt to taste
1 dessertspoon butter

Cook nearly 1 hour, stirring often. Beat up 1 egg and just before serving, stir into the mixture. Serve in hot tureen with any roast.

BUTTER SAUCE FOR USE WITH VEGETABLES

1 oz butter
pinch salt
1 oz flour

Mix these into a smooth paste, and place in saucepan with half a pint of cold water, then bring to the boil, stirring all the while A richer sauce is made with milk instead of water.

AUSTRALIAN SALAD DRESSING

4 tablespoons butter
1 tablespoon flour
white pepper
3 eggs
1 teaspoon Colman's mustard
1 saltspoonful salt
1/2 cup vinegar

Melt butter in a saucepan. Add flour and stir until smooth; add a little milk, and let boil; then add other ingredients, and stir until it thickens like custard. Allow to get cold.

To freshen a withered lettuce, soak in plenty of cold water, drain, wrap in darnp newspaper, and refrigerate.

VEGETABLES

POTATO BALLS

Mash 1 lb potatoes with cream, 1/4 lb grated ham, a teaspoon of minced parsley, a shallot, also minced, 1/2 teaspoon each of salt, pepper, mace; bind all together with the yolks of 2 eggs. Mould into balls, fry in butter and serve with good brown gravy.

POTATO APPLES

Take 2 cups hot mashed potatoes, mix with 2 tablespoons butter, 1/3 cup grated cheese, 1/2 teaspoon salt, cayenne, nutmeg, 2 tablespoons cream, yolks of 2 eggs. Make into small balls, roll in flour, egg and breadcrumbs, and brown in boiling fat (deep fry and drain on paper towel).

POTATO CROQUETTES

Boil and peel 6 large potatoes; pass through a wire sieve into a basin; add 1 egg or yolks of 2, and season with black pepper and salt, mix well and let stand till nearly cold, then form into 12 or 14 balls. Roll them in flour, then in beaten egg, and breadcrumbs. Deep fry to a nice golden brown, then drain on paper towel.

When picnicking, add a good pinch of bicarbonate of soda to milk to keep it fresh all day corked.

POTATO SAUTEES

Boil new potatoes but do not let them get too soft. Cut into 1/4 inch slices, put in enamelled saucepan with butter, pepper, salt, and chopped parsley. Hold over fire and shake until each slice has parsley etc. all over it. Serve hot.

STUFFED POTATOES

Peel and take out most of the inside of some raw potatoes. Fill with mincemeat, chopped parsley, butter, pepper and salt. Put in a tin and bake until well cooked and light brown.

POTATO TURNOVERS

Mix about 1 pint of hot mashed potatoes with a beaten egg, season with salt and pepper, and roll it well in flour. Do not use too much flour. Form into balls, and press or roll out rather thin. Put a teaspoon of meat, minced and seasoned, on half, fold over, and press edges together. Have ready plenty of smoking hot oil and deep fry turnovers on both sides to pale brown. Drain on paper towel.

CAULIFLOWER

Place pieces of cooked cauliflower in piedish; cover with white sauce, sprinkle grated cheese over. Bake in oven hot enough to soften or melt cheese, for about 1/2 hour.

CAULIFLOWER AU GRATIN

1 cauliflower
butter
6 oz grated cheese
breadcrumbs
1/2 cup white sauce
cayenne pepper
1 tablespoon mustard

Boil cauliflower until fairly tender, then put in piedish quite flat; pour over it the white sauce, in which some of the cheese, mustard and cayenne have been mixed; put on the top the remainder of the cheese, butter and breadcmmbs, bake until a nice brown and serve hot.

SAVOURY TOMATOES

8 tomatoes
2-1/2 oz breadcrumbs
2 oz butter
pepper & salt
3 small rounds far bacon
1 oz grated cheese
8 rounds buttered toast

Squeeze out the seeds and fleshy portion, mix with crumbs, cheese, butter and seasoning, and fill tomatoes with the mixture. On each tomato place a round of fat bacon, then grill or bake for 6 minutes. Serve each tomato on buttered toast.

SAVOURY TOMATO

4 large tomatoes, sliced
3 carrots, sliced
pepper & salt
3 large onions
3 raw potatoes, quartered

Boil all together for an hour; thicken with flour and chopped parsley.

BAKED TOMATOES

Take 6 large tomatoes, cut off tops and scoop out centres. Have ready some minced meat, pepper, salt, and small onion; fill tomatoes with this mixture. Put tops on again and bake slowly till a nice brown.

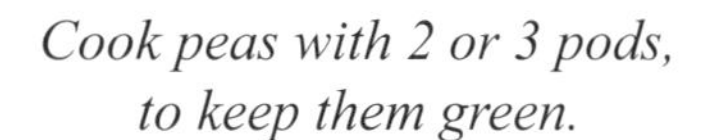

Cook peas with 2 or 3 pods, to keep them green.

STEWED CUCUMBERS

1 lb cucumbers
1 oz butter
1/2 lb onions
1 teaspoon flour

Peel the cucumbers and onions; cut in slices one eighth of an inch thick; fry in butter till well browned; put into a saucepan with 1/4 pint hot water or vegetable broth; season with pepper and salt; stew till quite soft; then add flour and butter well mixed together, and boil four or five minutes.

TASTY WAY OF COOKING MARROW

Cut up a vegetable marrow, and put in stewpan with butter or beef dripping; put pepper and salt between layers, and add 1 or 2 spring onions; cook very slowly. When cooked, take out pieces carefully, and serve with sauce made of the juice left, and thickened with flour.

STUFFED TOMATOES

7 good sized tomatoes
1-1/2 oz butter
2 oz ham
pepper and salt
1 dessertspoon parsley
2 oz breadcrumbs
shred of onion
7 fried strips of bread

Cut tops off tomatoes, scoop out part of inside; mix the parsley, very finely chopped breadcrumbs, ham and onion in a basin; season with pepper and salt, and bind together with butter. Fill tomatoes with this mixture; stand on a buttered tin, and bake 10 minutes. Have ready 7 rounds of fried bread. Stand tomatoes on, and serve.

BAKED CHOPS WITH TOMATO

Put in a pie dish layer of chops, then sliced tomatoes and onions, pepper and salt, then bacon and egg crumbs; continue this until dish is full. Bake 1 hour; serve with rich gravy.

STEWED CHOPS

1 oz butter
1/2 pint gravy
3 or 4 chops
1/2 oz flour
small piece onion

Put butter in saucepan; when melted stir in flour until smooth, then pour in water or gravy, stir till it boils, season with salt, add chops with fat cut off, and simmer gently for about 1 hour.

DEVILLED MUTTON

Slice cold mutton rather thinly. Rub over each slice with a piece of onion, and spread one side thickly with good chutney. Roll each up, dip into frying batter and fry in deep fat till a golden colour. Serve at once, dusted with cayenne and a dash of curry powder, in a tureen; serve a rich brown sauce, flavoured with shallot, chopped parsley and lemon rind.

CHOPS AND TOMATOES

Butter a saucepan, then put in a layer of sliced tomatoes, sprinkle with salt, pepper, and a little sugar. Then lay on slices of onion, then layer of chops. Do this until the dish is full, and allow it to simmer slowly for 2 hours, or, still better, put in a braising dish in the oven.

To coat food with flour or bread crumbs evenly and without a mess, shake in a plastic ice cream container instead of a plastic or paper bag.

Before putting stewing steak in fridge, cut it into cubes. When needed, you can put straight into pan without having to wait and thaw.

When cooking rice add a few drops of lemon juice, it improves the flavour and keeps the grains separated.

HARICOT MUTTON

1-1/2 Ib neck chops	*1 onion*
1 turnip	*1 pint stock or water*
1 oz dripping	*1 carrot*
1 oz flour	*chopped parsley*

Make the fat hot in a saucepan. Trim the chops, and fry brown both sides. Put on a plate. Slice onion into rings and fry till deep brown, sprinkle in the flour, pepper and salt; add stock. Stir till boiling. Boil 5 minutes. Strain onion out of gravy and return gravy to saucepan. Lay in the chops and stew gently 1/2 hour. Peel carrot and turnip, cut into neat half-inch pieces, add to saucepan, simmer gently 1 hour longer. Dish the chops into a circle with vegetables in centre. Pour gravy over and sprinkle with chopped parsley.

TONGUES IN JELLY

Cover six sheep's tongues in water, add 1 onion, carrot, spice, mace, cloves and pepper corns, and simmer 3 hours. Take out tongues and place in cold water. Skim, trim roots, and cut in halves lengthways.

To a pint of liquor add 1 oz of gelatine, salt and pepper to taste. Wet a mould, and lay in tongues and slices of hard boiled egg. Pour in liquor and stand till set.

EXETER STEW AND SAVOURY BALLS

1 lb lean beef
1 anion
2 tablespoons vinegar
pepper, salt to taste
2 oz dripping
2 tablespoons flour
2 pints cold water

Put dripping into a stewpan and brown chopped onion; add flour and brown that, then add water, pepper, salt and stir until it boils. Cut meat into small pieces and dip in vinegar. Place in stewpan and cover closely. Stew for 1-1/2 hours then add savoury balls, made as follows:

1/2 lb flour
1 teaspoon baking powder
parsley
4 oz suer
1 onion
pepper and salt

Chop finely suet, onion, and parsley, then add to the flour and powder with a little water. Cut dough into 12 pieces and roll into balls. Place on top of stew and cook for 3/4 hour.

If you grease the cup in which you measure honey,
treacle or syrup, every drop will
run out with no waste

MOCK DUCK

Take 1-1/2 Ib of steak; make a stuffing as for a turkey; spread on steak, roll it up and tie into shape of a duck. Roast for 3/4 hour in quick oven, and keep basting it well.

STEW

Cut 2 Ib beef meat in squares, add 2 carrots and 2 onions sliced, pepper and salt. Put in saucepan with 1 teaspoon of dripping, at side of slow fire. Let it simmer for 2 hours, and then thicken.

TO USE A SHIN OF BEEF

Shin of beef can be used in many ways. Beef slices from the best of the lean part. Beef stew served up with parsley sauce. Meat pie made in the same way as a beef steak pie. Beef pudding in basins much improved by addition of an ox kidney cut up finely. Also brawn. For pie stand the dish on the stove to stew slowly for several hours. For brawn, stew the bones with what is left of the meat until the meat and gristle falls off the bones. The liquor makes splendid stock. Add stock liberally to the brawn, season with sage, pepper, salt and nutmeg. Anything made from the shin of beef must be stewed a long time gently.

BRAWN

One knuckle, 2 sheep's tongues, 1 lb gravy beef, and little pickled pork; boil about two hours, or till the meat comes off the bone. Remove all bones and cut finely. Add marjoram, parsley, pepper and salt. Fill the moulds, then add liquor from the meat with a little gelatine to set.

VEAL BRAWN

Boil a knuckle of veal until tender, skim well, add a carrot and onion. Take out the meat, add teaspoon mace, peppercorns, cloves and a little salt. Boil liquor again. Cut meat small, add liquor, put into mould.

VEAL SHAPE

1-1/2 lb veal
1 slice ham
pepper & salt
1 lemon
3 hard boiled eggs

Stew the meat with the thin rind of lemon in very little water until quite tender; when done, cut up both veal and ham into small pieces. Mince lemon rind very fine and set aside to cool. Add lemon juice and seasonings with stock, and let cool. Slice eggs, arrange in plain mould or dish. Pour in cold stock and meat, set aside until cold, when it should turn out whole. An excellent breakfast dish.

POTTED MEAT

Cold meat with a little cold bacon or tongue minced up, breadcrumbs, salt, pepper, ground mace to taste, mixed with stock. Press into jar, and steam for an hour; when nearly cold, turn out.

BRAISED FOWL

Stuff with pork sausages. Put into saucepan with a tablespoon of butter or good dripping; sprinkle with pepper and salt. Put on low heat and let it cook very slowly for 2-1/2 hours, turning carefully until all sides are browned. Make a good brown gravy after the fowl has been removed. Fowls cooked this way are much nicer and moister than when roasted.

CHEESE AND BACON LOAF

6 tablespoons soft margarine
2 cups S.R. flour
1 teaspoon dry mustard
1/4 teaspoon pepper
4 rashers bacon chopped finely
3/4 cup grated cheddar cheese
2/3 cup milk
1 teaspoon baking powder
1/2 teaspoon salt
1 egg

Put all the ingredients together in a large bowl and stir until they are well mixed. Grease a 1/2kg loaf tin and put the mixture into it. Cook in a moderately hot oven for 45 minutes or until well risen and golden brown. Leave in the tin for a few minutes before turning out. Serve sliced and buttered when cold. This is also good for a light lunch with cheese, tomatoes and soup.

RABBIT IN WHITE WINE

1 rabbit, jointed and dredged with 1 tablespoon flour, and seasoned with salt and freshly ground pepper
2 tablespoons olive oil
10 small white onions (spring)
2 rashers bacon diced, OR 4 teaspoons bacon bits
1 cup dry white wine or dry cider
1/2 cup water
1 sprig thyme
1 garlic clove crushed
2 tablespoons snipped chives
1 tablespoon tomato paste
1 bay leaf
500g button mushrooms

Heat oil and saute rabbit until pieces are golden, place in casserole dish and keep warm. Put the tiny onions in the pan with the bacon (if using) and saute until onions are just coloured. Add to rabbit. Add the wine and then the water which has been mixed with tomato paste. Add herbs, garlic and chives, season and add a little extra freshly ground pepper. Cover and cook gently for about an hour until rabbit is tender. Just before rabbit is done, toss in the mushrooms. Remove to serving dish, or be lazy like me and serve directly from casserole. Sprinkle liberally with parsley. Stand back and wait for the applause.

KROMESKIES OF RABBIT

1 lb cooked rabbit
butter
frying fat
slices cold boiled bacon
seasoning
1 egg

Mince rabbit, season and moisten with beaten egg. Roll into shapes size of cork; wrap each shape in slice of bacon cut thin. (Make batter with 1/4 lb flour, 1 egg, milk). Dip kromeskies in batter and fry in hot fat (deep fry). Drain and pile on hot dish.

When making junket, dissolve the tablet in vanilla essence instead of water to improve taste.

DRUNKEN BUNNY

1 rabbit
1 large carrot diced
1 teaspoon sugar
1 large onion sliced finely
1 cup of beer
mixed herbs
2 rashers bacon OR 4 teaspoons bacon bits
1 tablespoon olive or maize oil
1 teaspoon Dijon mustard
1 teaspoon arrowroot mixed with 2 tablespoons water (optional)
plenty of finely chopped parsley

If using a non stick fry pan, oil is not necessary. Brown rabbit in hot oil. Remove to casserole dish. Put onion, carrot and bacon in fry pan, put on lid and let vegetables sweat for about 7 minutes. Lift out rabbit and put vegetables in bottom of casserole, then rabbit on top. Season with salt & pepper, and pour the beer over, add sugar. herbs and mustard.
Bring to the boil. cover the pot and allow to simmer on a very low heat for 1-1/2 hours until rabbit is very tender. If necessary thicken with arrowroot or flour & water. Sprinkle liberally with parsley.

RABBIT

Joint a young rabbit, slice 2 fair sized onions, add salt and pepper to taste, 3/4 cup water; stew gently for 1 hour. Turn into a round dish. add 1 cup milk, 1-1/2 cups bread crumbs. 2 slices bacon. 1 tablespoon dried marjoram, 1 tablespoon thyme. Cover dish and bake slowly for 1 hour.

TASTY WAY OF COOKING RABBIT

1 rabbit
pepper & salt
sauce if liked
1/4 lb bacon
1 cup clear stock

Joint rabbit, cut up bacon and put alternate layers of each in a jam jar; add pepper and salt, sauce, then cup of stock. Cover jar and cook in very slow oven for several hours. Turn out when cold and serve.

BROWNED RABBIT

Cut up rabbit into joints, sprinkle with seasoning and flour. Fry till well browned, then put in stew pan and simmer for 2 hours.

RABBIT RISSOLES

One cup mashed potato, 1/2 cup flour, pepper and salt; 1/2 cup diced rabbit, mix with 1 egg; fry in boiling fat (deep fry).

CHICKEN MOULD

Line a mould with aspic jelly, hard boiled egg, parsley, and green peas. When this is set, fill it with slices of cold boiled chicken, ham, and tongue, and pour over this aspic until quite full. Turn out when set, and garnish with lettuce or parsley. Aspic: one pint stock to 1 oz; gelatine, mixed herbs, peppercorns, allspice, salt and pepper to taste. Put into saucepan and let come to the boil Strain through muslin.

CHICKEN ROLL

1/2 lb cold chicken
salt & pepper to taste
grated lemon rind
1/2 lb ham or bacon.
minced parsley
4 oz seasoned boiled rice

Bind with a beaten egg and form into a roll; tie round with greased paper, and bake for 20 minutes. Serve with rich brown gravy and garnish with lemon slices.

COTTAGE PIE (COLD MEAT)

Mince any kind of cold meat, put into a pie dish to about 1-1/2 inches deep. Cover with gravy, add salt and pepper. Cover with mashed potatoes, smooth across the top, mark the top with a knife (diamond shape) and bake till crisp and brown.

KANGAROO STEAMED

Procure a young kangaroo, let it hang for a few days to dry well. Then cutoff the tail, bone the kangaroo, and put the bones on to boil well for gravy. ('The tail is nice if boiled in stock to make soup). Cut trimmed flesh into neat square pieces, flour well and season with salt and pepper. Cut up some slices of bacon in small dice; make a seasoning as for veal and roll into small balls. Add a little finely cut onion if liked. Place in a jar a layer of the kangaroo pieces, then a layer of bacon, then a layer of the seasoned balls. Repeat this until you have placed the quantity you require to cook; then pour over this the gravy. Place the jar in water up to the neck, tie down and keep quite closed, and steam it for 3 or 4 hours. Serve with red currant jelly. It is better to prepare this the day before cooking it, so as to have the goodness from the bones for gravy.
Kangaroo is also very nice finely cut and well seasoned, and made into pats, dipped in well beaten eggs, seasoned, and then bread crumbs, well seasoned all over, fried in plenty of hot beef dripping.

POTTED LENTIL SAVOURY

1/4 1b lentils (cooked)
2 oz bread crumbs
chopped parsley
salt & pepper
3 oz mashed potato
1 egg (beaten)
a little onion juice
1 oz butter

Put all in a pan, mix well together, stirring all the time. When cooked, turn into a mortar, pound well, and press into potting dishes, and melt butter over the top. This makes excellent sandwiches with a little mustard spread on.

DORNIERS

Minced cold meat, rice (boiled), little sage and onion (cooked), pepper and salt, few bread crumbs and an egg. Mix and make into patties. Fry in batter in plenty of fat (deep fry).

A butcher's shop in Franklin, Tasmania, in the early 1900s.

The water driven mill at North Franklin, Tasmania, where settlers took their wheat.

Centre pages: A panorama of Port Arthur during convict occupation. A total of 16

ıvicts were transported to Australia, the last shipment being to Fremantle in 1840

Salamanca Place and the wharf at Hobart in 1856.

A cell gallery in the Port Arthur penitentiary.

CURRY PASTIES

Take some cold meat (free it from skin, fat and gristle), mince and season with pepper, salt and curry powder. Mash some potatoes with an egg, season with pepper and salt. Line patty tins with potato; fill with meat; cover with potato again, ornament the edges, brush with milk and bake in quick oven.

SALMIS OF COLD MEAT

Cut up in small square dice 2 oz each of carrot, turnip, celery, onion. Add 1/4 lb streaky bacon, 20 peppercorns, 5 cloves, a small piece of mace, 1/2 a bay leaf, sprig of thyme and marjoram. Put in a saucepan 2 oz butter or dripping. Fry all ingredients till brown, add 1-1/2 tablespoons flour, add 1-1/2 pints stock or water, small gherkin chopped fine with salt to taste. Simmer 20 minutes; take off fat; strain; put liquor in a clean saucepan; add any kind of finely cut cold meat; simmer 20 minutes. Serve with toast snippets.

FRICASEE OF COLD ROAST BEEF

slices of beef
pepper & salt
1 onion
yolks 2 eggs
a piece of butter or gravy
parsley
cup water
teaspoon vinegar

Cut the beef into thin slices; season well with pepper, salt and parsley; add onion chopped very fine. Put all together into a stewpan with a piece of butter or gravy, a large cupful of water, and simmer gently. Just before serving add yolks of two eggs, well beaten, and a teaspoon vinegar. Stir briskly and serve with baked potatoes.

POTATO TURNOVERS

Mince any kind of cold meat, moisten with a little gravy. Make a paste of cold potatoes, with enough flour to roll. Put the meat in squares, and fold up in the shape of a turnover. Fry slowly in a little dripping.

SAVOURY PYRAMIDS

These delicious little dainties can be made with any odd pieces of meat; beef, mutton, lamb, pork or veal, no matter how small as long as they are perfectly sweet and free from fat, bone and gristle. Break 3 eggs in basin, beat until light; then stir in by degrees 6 tablespoons fine breadcrumbs, 3 oz slightly melted butter, 1 tablespoon finely cut parsley, 1 teaspoon mixed herbs, salt, a little grated lemon peel, pinch of cayenne, 3/4 lb finely chopped meat; just enough good gravy to moisten the whole. Mix ingredients thoroughly and shape in little pyramids, egg them entirely over, sprinkle with breadcrumbs. Bake in greased tin for 1/2 hour in well heated oven. Serve on a hot dish.

POOR MAN'S PUDDING

Cut up the meat from a cold joint; put bones on to boil for gravy. grate up any piece of bread that may be left, say a plateful of breadcrumbs; a similar quantity of grated cheese, slice an onion thin as a wafer; peel about 4 potatoes and cut in rather thick slices. Cut or mince 4 pieces of cold meat, sprinkle with flour, season with pepper and salt, then have a greased piedish. Put in a layer of sliced potatoes, sprinkle a little onion on, then put a layer of the seasoned meat. Sprinkle some grated cheese on the meat, then put on a layer of breadcrumbs, and again a layer of sliced potatoes and onion, then meat and cheese and breadcrumbs. If that fills your piedish, then put in the gravy. Bake for an hour or a little longer; if your oven is rather hot, place an old dish on top of the piedish and remove it in time to brown the pie. This is a very good way to use up cold meat and the hard part of cheese, and pieces of bread; raw potatoes are better for this than those previously cooked, there is more flavour in them.

BACON DISH

Lay slices of bacon between slices of bread; cut to the same size, press together and dip in batter made of egg, milk, and a little flour to thicken. Fry for 10 minutes and serve very hot.

SAVOURY BALLS FOR STEWS

1/2 lb flour
1 teaspoon baking powder
1/2 teaspoon salt
1/4 teaspoon pepper
sweet herbs if liked
1/2 an onion, chopped
3 tablespoons chopped suet
1 tablespoon chopped parsley

Put flour in basin, mix with other ingredients to a very stiff paste. Drop into gravy when the stew has been cooking for an hour and a half. Cook for 3/4 hour. Arrange balls around dish, and put meat and gravy in centre.

RISSOLES

1/2 lb meat, minced
1 oz dripping
small amount water/stock
salt & pepper
beaten egg
1 small onion, chopped
1 tablespoon flour
1 dessert spoon Worcestershire sauce
breadcrumbs

If fresh meat is used, fry a nice brown, then melt dripping in pan and fry onion; sprinkle with flour, add water or stock gradually. Mix in meat, add seasoning, form into rissoles, coat with egg and crumbs. Deep fry for 3 minutes. Turn out on paper.

SHEPHERD'S PIE

Mince 1/2 lb cold meat, season with pepper and salt, put into greased piedish and pour 1/4 pint gravy over it. Partly boil and chop an onion, add to meat. Mash some potatoes and spread over meat like a crust. Finish it with a fork, and bake in hot oven about 20 minutes until nicely browned.

ECONOMICAL RISSOLES

Mash 1 lb cold potatoes with 1 oz melted butter; add pepper and salt, 2 tablespoons finely minced meat, 1 dessertspoon tomato sauce. Mix to a paste with a well beaten egg, form into rissoles, dip in beaten egg and breadcmmbs, and fry to a golden brown.

TOAD IN A HOLE

1/2 lb sausages/cold meat
2 eggs
1/4 lb flour
1/2 pint milk
seasoning

Grease a tin, put in meat, make batter of flour, eggs and milk, beat well, add seasoning, and pour over meat. Bake for 1 hour.

TOMATO HASH

Butter a dish well, put in layer of sliced tomatoes, a layer of cold meat sliced thin, then a layer of bread and butter, and so on until the dish is full. Season with pepper and salt, beat 2 eggs and pour over top. Bake brown.

CAMBRIDGE CROQUETTES

Make a paste with equal parts of flour and cold mashed potatoes, a little dripping and a pinch of salt. Mix into a stiff dough with either milk or water. Roll out thinly. Cut into squares for turnovers and fill with mincemeat seasoned to taste. Deep fry till a nice brown, or for about 20 minutes.

A NICE BREAKFAST DISH

A few slices ham
1/2 lb cold potatoes
cayenne pepper
butter
4 eggs

Mash potatoes and line a buttered pieddish with them. Cut the ham into small squares, put on top of potatoes and sprinkle with cayenne. Bake 15 minutes. Break eggs into it without breaking yolks. Then bake until eggs are cooked.

KIDNEY ON TOAST

3 or 4 sheep's kidneys
salt
cayenne
buttered toast
1 egg
butter
parsley

Chop kidneys very finely, season with salt, cayenne pepper and chopped parsley. Place in saucepan with small piece butter. Stir over fire until done; add well beaten egg yolk and a little lemon juice. Spread on hot buttered toast and serve hot.

A LUNCHEON RELISH

Melt and brown 2 tablespoons butter, add 1 sliced onion, cook until delicately browned; add 2 tablespoons of flour and brown, stirring all the while; then add 2 cups finely chopped meat; add 1 cup stock, salt and pepper to taste, 1 cup tomatoes, and cook until thoroughly heated. Season and serve on hot dish with small moulds of boiled rice.

CORNISH PASTIES

1/2 lb beef steak, 1 sheep's kidney, cut fine, 1 good sized potato, 1 small onion, minced. Cut meat and potato into dice, mix with onion, sprinkle salt and pepper over, mix welL

Make short pastry from 10 oz flour, 2-1/2 oz lard, 2-1/2 oz dripping, large 1/2 teaspoon baking powder, and cold water to mix. Turn pastry on board, cut into as many pieces as are needed; roll pastry into rounds, put on some meat mixture with about 1 teaspoon cold water. Gather edges of pastry together, along the top of pasty, and prick with fork. Bake in a moderate oven 1/2 hour. (Try potatoes with skewer and if done, meat will be done also).

Tissues and paper towels are ideal for draining fried foods before serving.

The following recipe was first published in 1867. It is nor intended to be used, but is included for its interest.

COLD PARTRIDGE PIE

Bone partridges - the number according to the size the pie is wanted, make some good force, and fill the partridges with it, put a whole raw truffle in each partridge (let the truffle be peeled); raise the pie, lay a few slices of veal in the bottom, and a thick layer of force; then the partridges, and four truffles to each partridge; then cover the partridges and truffles over with sheets of bacon, cover the pie in and finish it. It will take four hours baking. Cut two pounds of lean ham (if eight partridges are in the pie) into very thin slices, put it in a stewpan along with the bones and giblets of the partridges, and any other loose giblets that are at hand, an old fowl, a faggot of thyme and parsley, a little mace, and about twenty-four shalots; add about a pint of stock. Set the stewpan on a stove to draw down for half an hour, then put three quarts of good stock; let it boil for two hours, then strain it off, and reduce the liquid to one pint; add sherry wine to it, and put aside till the pie is baked. When the pie has been out of the oven for half an hour, boil the residue strained from the bones, &c., of the partridges, and put it into the pie. Let it stand for twenty-four hours before it is eaten. - N.B. Do not take any of the fat from the pie, as that is what preserves it. A pie made in this manner will be eatable for three months after it is cut; in short, it cannot spoil in any reasonable time. All cold pies are made in this manner.

IRISH STEW

2 brown onions
4 turnips
6 oz split lentils
1 pint water
4 carrots
8 potatoes of good size
2 oz butter
pepper and salt

Cut the vegetables into thin slices; put the water, butter, and seasoning in stewpan with the carrots; when boiling add the turnips, onions and lentils, with the potatoes on top. Stew gently tor 3/4 hour.

MEAT PASTE

Cold meat with little cold bacon or tongue minced twice, salt, pepper, ground mace to taste, mixed with stock. Press into jar, and use with bread and butter.

RAISED PORK PIES

To 3 lb flour allow 1-1/4 Ib lard or dripping, and enough milk to cover fat. Boil fat and water together, and stir into the flour. Leave for about 20 minutes; then work into shape, and fill with meat, pepper, and salt; then cover, joining edges well together. A quick oven to set the paste; then slower for about 3 hours. When nearly done, brush with egg. The above quantity will make 3 fair sized pies.

SAUSAGE ROLLS

6 oz flour
3 oz butter
1/2 egg yolk
sausages

Rub butter into flour till like breadcmmbs, put 1/2 yolk into cold water, and then mix in with spoon; then with the hand roll paste out, cut in squares. In centre of each piece place sausage, roll crust over, place in oven and bake 20 minutes. Brush over with white of egg before quite cooked.

Before heating milk, rinse the saucepan with cold water, this helps prevent milk from sticking to the bottom of the pan.

ANGEL PUDDING

2 oz flour
2 eggs
few drops of lemon essence
2 oz butter
1/2 pint boiling milk

Beat eggs, flour, and sugar to taste, together; then pour on the boiling milk, beating all the time. Place in buttered piedish and bake in quick oven 1/2 hour.

BAKED PLUM PUDDING

8 oz flour
raisins
2 oz peel
1 large teaspoon baking powder
1 egg
4 oz suet
3 oz sugar
1/2 teaspoon nutmeg
1/4 pint milk

Mix flour, powder, pinch salt; shred and chop suet; stone raisins and chop; grate nutmeg; mix egg with milk, and stir in other mixture. Spread evenly over a baking dish. Bake at once in quick oven for about 1/2 hour. Dust with castor sugar and serve.

BAKED JAM ROLL

1 lb flour
water
stiff jam
1/2 lb dripping
1 teaspoon baking powder

Rub the fat into the flour; add baking powder, pinch of salt, and water to make a dough. Roll out the pastry, spread with a stiff jam, form into roly poly; join edges at the ends and put in a baking tin with joined edge down. Bake in a good oven. Serve hot or cold, with castor sugar sprinkled over.

Liquid added slowly and not mixed evenly causes scones to be leathery

CREAM PUDDING

Put into a double saucepan 3 cups of milk; put on to scald; mix 5 tablespoons of flour into a smooth paste with 1 cup of milk; pour a little hot milk into paste; stir all back into saucepan quickly; put on to boil. stirring till quite thick; add a good sized piece of butter; sweeten to taste. Take off fire. add 1 well beaten egg; boil all 1/4 hour, put into wet mould and leave till cold. Turn out. and serve stewed fruit.

DUCHESS OF YORK PUDDING

Two eggs, their weight in flour, and in butter, and in sugar. Beat butter to cream, with sugar. Add eggs, well beaten; stir in flour, then two tablespoons raspberry jam; beat in 1/2 teaspoon carb soda. Grease a mould; put in pudding leaving plenty of room to rise. Cover with greased paper. and steam about 2 hours.

ESTY HASY PUDDING

1 cup flour

1 tablespoon butter

1/2 cup milk

1 teaspoon baking powder

scant 3/4 cup sugar

1 egg

Put preferred jam in piedish, pour mixture in and bake in quick oven for 1/2 hour.

FIVE MINUTES PUDDING

Put 2 oz flour and 1-1/2 oz sugar into a basin. Make a hole in flour, and break in 2 eggs, and beat well. Add a tablespoon of baking powder and pour at once into a tin lined with greased paper, and bake for about 5 minutes. Try with a skewer. Turn on to a sugared board, spread raspberry jam on quickly, and roll up at once. Sift sugar over.

FRENCH APPLE PUDDING

Melt 1-1/2 oz butter; stir into it until quite smooth, 2 oz flour, and stir in gradually 3/4 pint milk. Boil 3 minutes, pour into basin, and add 1 oz sugar, and 1/2 teaspoon vanilla; beat in 2 eggs. Put a thick layer of stewed apples in a piedish, pour batter over, and bake 40 minutes.

GINGER PUDDING

2 cups flour
a little salt
1/2 cup chopped raisins
1/2 cup milk
1 teaspoon carb soda
2 teaspoons ground ginger
1/2 cup treacle
1 tablespoon melted butter

Boil 2 hours.

QUEEN PUDDING

1/2 pint breadcrumbs
yolks 2 eggs
1 oz butter
1 pint milk
2 oz sugar
essence to taste

Bake in a piedish, then put a thin layer of jam on top. Beat egg whites with little sugar to a stiff froth, with essence of lemon. Spread it over the jam, then brown slightly, and serve.

YORKSHIRE PUDDING

1-1/2 pints milk
3 eggs
6 large tablespoons flour
little salt

Put flour in a basin, add salt and stir in enough milk to make stiff batter. When perfectly smooth, add remainder of milk and eggs, well beaten. Pour into shallow tin well rubbed with beef dripping. Bake in oven for 1 hour; cut pudding into small square pieces and serve from heated dish.

SWEET CRUST

With 6 oz fine breadcrumbs, mix intimately 4 oz castor sugar- that is the entire material for the crust. Arange in a deep piedish, say, 1-1/4 lb apples, peeled and cored, and sweetened with 4 oz sugar; then spread the mixture of breadcrumbs and sugar over the surface. Bake in quick oven 3/4 hour. The crumbs and sugar combine with heat and moisture to form firm crust, which is as good to eat cold as hot. Other fruit can be substituted for apples, and to prevent the crumb and sugar mixture dropping into the spaces between plums or gooseberries, separation is provided by covering the surface of the fruit with bread sliced thin.

COCOA PUDDING

Boil 1/2 lb light stale bread in 1 pint of milk, stirring continually until it becomes a thick paste; then add 1 oz butter, 1/2 lb sugar, and 2 teaspoons of cocoa, with a few drops of vanilla. Take off fire and mix in first the yolks, then the whites, beaten to a strong froth, of two eggs. Put in a buttered dish, and bake 3/4 hour in moderate oven.

COTTAGE PUDDING

Warm 2-1/2 tablespoons of butter; stir in a cup of white sugar, 1 well-beaten egg; put 2 teaspoons of cream tartar into a pint of flour; add 1 teaspoon carb soda in a cup of milk, flavoured with nutmeg or lemon. Bake 3/4 hour in a slow oven. Serve with sweet sauce.

DATE PUDDING

Butter a piedish; put dates round, grate breadcrumbs to about half fill the dish; beat two eggs, a little flour, a pint of milk, tablespoonof sugar, beat together; pour over crumbs; bake till set.

GARIBALDI CREAM

4 cups water
2 lemons
4 tablespoons sugar
4 eggs
4 tablespoons arrowroot

Boil rind of lemon, cut very thin, in water for 20 minutes; remove from fire; take out peel, and add juice of lemons and sugar; thicken with arrowroot, and boil till clear. Have ready whites of eggs, whisked well, and beat smoothly into the boiled arrowroot. Pour half of it into a border mould, and colour the other half either pink or yellow. Fill up centre with clear jelly of another colour.

ITALIAN CREAM

Dissolve 1 oz gelatine in 1 quart of milk; add well-beaten yolks of 3 eggs, 1 cup sugar, piece of lemon; let all just come to the boil; then take it from the stove, and when almost cold stir in the whites of the eggs (which have been beaten to a froth); flavour with vanilla. Pour into a wetmould. Turn out, when cold, and serve with custard.

STRAWBERRY CREAM

Rub 1 pint of strawberries through a sieve; add 1 quart whipped cream, 3/4 Ib white sugar, and freeze.

TRIFLE

1 Madeira cake
1 quart custard
apricot jam
essence
4 bananas
1/2 pint whipped cream
few almonds

Cut cake into slices; put into a dish; then layers of fruit and cake, with the jam on top, until the dish is full. Pour the custard (hot) over the top; then add whipped cream, and place almonds over the trifle.

To give an apple pie a delicious flavour, add juice of 2 oranges and a little cinnamon instead of water.

SANDWICHES

Use pastry cutters to cut sandwiches into fancy shapes for a child's birthday party. You'll find it easier when the bread has been refrigerated for a short while.

FILLING FOR SANDWICH

2 tablespoons table sugar
2 tablespoons boiling water
2 tablespoons butter

Put water on sugar and let stand for a while, then add butter and beat. Sometimes it will take 20 minutes to become like cream.

ORANGE CHEESE

1/4 lb butter
grated rind of 2 oranges
strained juice of 3 oranges
1 lb sugar
3 eggs

Beat eggs, add sugar, beat for a minute, stir in the grated rind and strained juice. Put in a basin with butter and place over boiling water, stir with a wooden spoon until the mixture is as thick as honey. Pour in warm dry jars, and seal securely. Stored in airtight jars and put in cool dry place, will keep for weeks.

CHEESE SANDWICHES

1 hard-boiled egg
salt and pepper
1 tablespoon vinegar
1/4 lb grated cheese
1 tablespoon melted butter

Mix all together well, and spread between buttered bread.

CHICKEN SANDWICHES

Mince up fine any cold chicken. Put into a saucepan. with gravy. Add a good piece of butter, a pinch of pepper and salt. Work very smooth while heating until it looks like a paste. When cold spread between slices of buttered bread.

"LEFT OVER" SANDWICHES

Brush the sandwiches with egg. Cover with breadcrumbs, and fry a nice brown in boiling oil or fat. Drain well and serve with finely chopped parsley.

Butter your sponge cake lightly before spreading with jam. This prevents the jam from soaking inro the sponge.

CAKES, SLICES & BISCUITS

VIENNA ICING

2 dessertspoons butter
5 ozs icing sugar
2 dessertspoons sherry OR coffee OR chocolate

Mix together for sponge icing, also for piping.

SNOWBALLS

1 cup sugar
1 cup water
1 oz gelatine

Soak gelatine in water till dissolved. Boil altogether for 8 minutes, cool just a little and add small cup of icing sugar. Beat until stiff, then roll in chocolate coconut.

TOFFEE

1 cup white sugar
1/2 cup water
1 dessertspoon vinegar
6 almonds (chopped)

Put the sugar and water in a saucepan and, when beginning to boil add vinegar and almonds. Boil until it will snap in cold water.

As the forest was cleared, the land was settled.

Early roadways through the southern Tasmanian forest.

CHOCOLATE MINT SLICE

1-1/2 cups S.R. flour
1/2 cup brown sugar
1 cup coconut
185 gm butter

FILLING

1-1/2 cups icing sugar
1-1/2 tablespoons milk
1/2 teaspoons peppermint essence - or to taste

TOPPING

1/2 cup drinking chocolate
90 gm copha

Mix all dry ingredients together and melt the butter. Pour onto dry ingredients and mix well. Press into a greased 28 x 18 cm shallow tray. Bake at 200 deg celsius for 15 - 20 minutes. While still warm spread with the peppermint filling.

FILLING

Sift icing sugar into a bowl. Melt copha. Blend in milk and peppermint essence and stir into icing sugar. Spread over base and allow to set.

TOPPING

Combine melted copha and drinking chocolate. Cool slightly and pour over the slice. Leave to set before cutting into fingers for serving.

LORETTA'S CHRISTMAS SLICE

1 pkt cherries - 4 ozs
1 pkt cashew nuts
90 gm copha
250 gm chocolate
3/4 cup toasted coconut
1 teaspoon instant coffee

Melt chocolate and copha together. Layer chocolate, coconut, fruit and nuts, coconut and chocolate. Smooth top. Set in refrigerator. Cut into fingers to serve. Leave out for a few minutes before cutting.

Biscuits will keep fresh and crisp if you put a teaspoon of sugar in your tin.

LEMON GINGER BISCUIT SLICE

4 ozs sugar
4 ozs butter
grated rind of 1 lemon
1/4 cup chopped glace ginger
up to 1/2 lb crushed Sweet biscuits
2 level tablespoons coconut
1 tablespoon lemon juice
1 beaten egg

Place the butter, sugar, coconut and lemon juice in a saucepan and stir until well mixed. Cook for 2 minutes. Remove from the heat and cool slightly, then add the grated lemon rind, the beaten egg, chopped ginger and enough crushed biscuits to make a good consistency.
Press firmly into a greased 7 inch sandwich tin and chill until firm. Cover the top with lemon flavoured glace icing and sprinkle with coconut. Cut into finger sized pieces to serve.

CHOCOLATE BALLS

1 -2/3 cups icing sugar
1 tablespoon coffee
3/4 cup coconut
4 ozs butter
3/4 cup rolled oats
cooking chocolate

Put rolled oats through blender. Cream butter and icing sugar. Mix in other ingredients. Roll in small balls and refrigerate until set. Melt chocolate in double saucepan and then dip balls in melted chocolate and top with glace cherry or walnut pieces.

KISSES

1/2 lb butter
1 cup sugar
2 eggs
3 cups S. R. flour

Cream butter and sugar, add eggs and mix well. Add other ingredients, roll out thin and cut out with biscuit cutter. Bake in a quick oven. Cool on racks. Stick together with raspberry jam and top with icing. Sprinkle with 100s and 1000s.

CUSTARD CREAMS

3 tablespoons flour
6 tablespoons sugar
1/4 lb butter
1 large or 2 small eggs
6 tablespoons custard powder
1 teaspoon baking powder

Cream butter and sugar, add eggs and beat well. Add flour, custard powder and baking powder sifted together. Make into stiff paste and put through biscuit forcer.

CHOCOLATE BISCUITS (NO COOKING)

1 pkt milk arrowroot biscuits, crushed
1 cup coconut
1/4 lb melted copha
3 tablespoons cocoa
1 tin condensed milk

Place crushed biscuits, coconut, cocoa and condensed milk in bowl and mix thoroughly. Add melted copha and mix thoroughly again. Roll into small balls, flatten and roll in coconut. Place in refrigerator until firm.

SUNBEAMS

1-1/2 cups flour
1/2 teaspoon carb soda
1 egg
a little milk
1 tablespoon sugar
1/41b butter
1 teaspoon cream of tartar

Rub butter into dry ingredients and mix with the beaten egg and enough milk to bind. Roll out and spread with raspberry jam. Make like roly poly and cut into rings. Bake in moderate oven 10-15 minutes.

Flour shaken on top of a cake to be iced will prevent icing from running over rhe sides of the cake.

After stewing apples, save juice and use instead of milk in scones, for a different flavour. Use it cold.

COCONUT MACAROONS

Whisk the whites of two fresh eggs until stiff. Then add 6 ozs sugar and beat until firm enough to keep shape. Then stir (not beat) in 4 ozs coconut. Place in spoonfuls on greased paper and bake in a cool oven until firm and lightly coloured, which can be anything from 20 to 45 minutes.

POWDER PUFFS

3 eggs
1 tablespoon boiling water

Beat for 5 minutes, then add 3/4 cup of sugar. Beat well. Sift together 3/4 cup arrowroot, 1 heaped tablespoon plain flour, 1/2 teaspoon carb or soda, and 1 teaspoon cream of tartar. Mix into egg mixture. Bake in teaspoonsfull on hot buttered slide for 2 minutes. Roll in icing sugar while hot. Put together with cream some hours before serving.

MARSHMALLOW SLICE

1 cup S.R. flour
1 cup coconut
4 ozs butter
3/4 cup light brown sugar
3 weetbix

Mix all dry ingredients and crushed weetbix. Melt butter and add to rest of ingredients. Press into greased lamington tin and bake 20 minutes in moderate oven. Take out and spread with raspberry jam while hot if desired.

THISTLEDOWN SPONGE

4 eggs
3/4 cup sugar
essence to taste
1/2 cup arrowroot
1/2 teaspoon carb soda
1 teaspoon cream of tartar

Beat eggs and sugar 15 minutes, then add sifted arrowroot and raisings and beat another 10 minutes. Add essence and beat again. Put in tins, which must not be greased, and bake 15 minutes in moderate oven. This sponge is delicious, but the directions must be followed closely.

GINGER SPONGE

1 cup flour
4 eggs
1 teaspoon cocoa
1/2 teaspoon carb soda
1 teaspoon cream of tartar
1 teaspoon cinnamon
3/4 cup sugar
2 teaspoons golden syrup
1 teaspoons ground ginger

Beat eggs and sugar first, then add golden syrup, beating well. Add flour etc, sifted. Lastly add 1 tablespoon hot water. Bake in moderate oven for 20 minutes.

SPONGE LILLIES

3 eggs
1 cup S. R. flour
1 cup sugar

Separate yolks and whites of eggs. Beat the yolks a little then add sugar and beat until white and creamy. Whip the whites until stiff, add to yolks & sugar, and mix until well blended. Stir in lightly the sifted flour. Drop in teaspoons full on a greased baking tray, allowing room to spread. Bake in a fairly hot oven until pale brown. They must not be allowed to bake until crisp. As each is removed from oven, roll into poke shape. When cold fill with whipped cream and place a piece of jelly in centre of each top.

SNOWBALLS

3 ozs butter
1 egg
1/2 cup sugar
1 teaspoon cream of tartar
1/2 cup milk
1 cup flour
1/2 teaspoon carb soda

Cream butter and sugar, add egg and milk, then flour and raisings. Cook in gem irons in moderate oven 10 - 15 minutes. When cold, ice with chocolate icing, split open and fill with cream.

CREAM PUFFS

Melt 1 heaped tablespoon butter then add 1/2 cup of boiling water. Place on stove and when mixture boils add 1/2 cup S.R. flour and stir quickly. Remove to mix then put back for a couple minutes. Add 2 unbeaten eggs one at a time. Beat until mixture is quite smooth. Place in teaspoons full on greased tray and bake in moderate oven for 30 minutes. When cool, split and fill with whipped cream.

QUEEN CAKES

3 cups S.R. flour
3/4 cup milk
1/2 lb butter
3 eggs
1 cup sugar
mixed fruits

Beat butter and sugar, add eggs then flour and fruit, lastly milk.
Put in paper cups and bake in moderate oven for 12-15 minutes.

PIKELETS

1 egg
2 ozs sugar
1/2 teaspoon carb soda
small 1/2 cup milk
1 teaspoon cream of tartar
2 cups flour

Beat egg with sugar, add milk then flour which has been sifted with raisings. Put in teaspoonsfull in buttered frying pan and cook slowly as they burn easily. When brown, turn. Cool on rack and then spread with butter and serve.

APPLE CAKE

1/21b butter
vanilla flavouring
1 teaspoon carb soda
1 tablespoon water
2 eggs
1-1/2 cups sugar
4 cups sifted flour
2 teaspoons cream of tartar

Cream butter and sugar, beat in eggs, water and essence. Then mix in flour sifted with raisings. Roll out 1/2 with plenty of flour, and cut into four pieces for easy handling. Put into large tin pressing joins together. Put up sides of tin. Spread well with cold stewed apples. Cover with remaining half of pastry and bake in moderate oven 20-30 minutes. Good iced with lemon icing, or with whipped cream for a dessert.

GEM SCONES

2 cups S.R. flour
3/4 cup milk
1 egg
2 tablespoons sugar
1 tablespoon butter

Beat sugar and butter together, add egg, milk and mix in the flour. Bake in hot greased gem irons in fairly hot oven for about 10 minutes. When cold, split and spread with butter.

CREAM CONES

Make some nice puff paste; have some little tins the shape of a cone; cut the pastry in strips and roll around the tin, and bake in a very quick oven. Slip the tins out and stand up the cases for pastry to cool. When quite cool, fill them with whipped cream and pile on dish, dusting them with sugar.

Scones are light if milk is at least room temperature. Warm if taken direct from refrigerator.

ALBERT BUNS

1/4 cup butter
1 egg
few currants
3 cups flour
1 teaspoon carb soda
1 cup sugar
1 cup milk
lemon essence
2 teaspoons cream tartar

Beat together butter, sugar and egg. Add milk, currants and essence, then mix in flour and raisings. Brush over with white of egg and sprinkle with sugar. Bake 15 - 20 minutes in moderate oven.

BUNS WITHOUT YEAST

Rub 1/4 lb butter or lard into 1 lb sifted flour, add 1/4 lb of currants and same of sugar, 2 oz candied peel, mixed spice to taste, some grated lemon rind, 3 beaten eggs, and 1 cup cold milk.
Divide into 12 parts, shape into buns, glaze with sugar and milk. Bake in moderate oven 15 or 20 minutes.

BATH BUNS

Rub 1/2 lb butter into 2 lb flour, 1/2 lb castor sugar and 2 oz finely chopped peel. Beat 3 eggs, warm 1/2 pint milk; mix all together, make into buns, then brush over with beaten egg and sprinkle with coarse sugar, some peel and a few carraway seeds on top when partly baked.

SHORTBREADS

Cream 2/3 cup butter with 1/4 cup castor sugar; add 1 egg. Stir in. 2-1/4 cups S.R. sifted flour & 3 teaspoons custard powder, then mix to dough consistency. Roll out, cut in fingers, then bake on greased tray 15 minutes in moderate oven.

COFFEE CAKE

2 eggs
2 cups flour
1 cup milk
2 teaspoons cream tartar
1 cup sugar
butter - walnut size piece
1 teaspoon carb soda

Mix the carb soda and cream tartar with the flour. Beat eggs, butter and sugar together; stir in flour gradually, adding milk last. Mix all well together, spread on buttered tin, and bake in quick oven for 20 minutes. Boil together in saucepan for 5 minutes: 3 tablespoons sugar, 1 butter, 1 cinnamon, 1 milk; and spread over cake.

CURRANT CAKE

1/2 lb butter
3 eggs
1/2 cup milk
1/4 lb currants
little lemon peel
2-1/2 reaspoons baking powder
1/2 lb sugar
2-1/2 cups flour
1/4 lb sultanas
few drops vanilla essence

Beat butter to a cream, add sugar and eggs; beat well together.
Add other ingredients mixed well; bake 1-1/2 hours in a steady oven.

A WINTER SALAD

Two large potatoes, passed through kitchen sieve,
Unwonted softness to the salad give;
Of mordant mustard add a single spoon
Distrust the condiment which bites so soon;
But deem it not, thou man of herbs, a fault
To add a double quantity of salt;
Three times the spoon with oil of Lucca crown,
And once with vinegar procured from town.
True flavour needs it, and your poet begs
The pounded yellow of two well-boiled eggs;
Let onion atoms lurk within the bowl,
And, scarce suspected, animate the whole;
And lastly, on the favoured compound toss
A magic teaspoon of anchovy sauce:
Then, though green turtle fail, though venison's rough,
And ham and turkey be nor boiled enough,
Serenely full, the epicure may say,
"Fate cannot harm me - I have dined to-day. "

CONVICTS

44. Every convict on his arrival at the Settlement is to be clothed in yellow or party-coloured clothing, and to be kept steadily and constantly at hard labour during the day with the gang to which he may be attached; no relaxation from actual hard labour shall be permitted until the convict shall have passed through at least one-third of the term for which he may have been sent to the Settlement; should he complete this period with good conduct, he may be removed to a gang, the labour of, which is of a lighter description, and he may at the discretion of the Commandant fill a situation, such as Sub-Overseer, Watchman, &c. In such situations he will be allowed to wear grey clothing, and should he discharge his duty satisfactorily, and complete another third of his period, with continued good conduct, he may be permitted to memorialize His Excellency for removal to the settled districts.

45. In the distribution among the different gangs regard is to be had to the character and disposition of each man, that the well disposed may be separated from the evil-minded, and those gangs which are composed of

men under local punishment, or whose general conduct is bad, are invarably to be selected for the most severe labour.

46. Every convict is to pay the most implicit obedience to the lawful commands of his superiors; if he shall consider himself aggrieved by any order, he is

No. 1. Ration.

FOR CONVICTS AT HARD LABOUR.

ARTICLES.	*No. of Days Weekly.*	*Scale ₩ Diem.* *lbs.*	*oz.*	*drs.*	ARTICLES.	*No. of Days Weekly.*	*Scale ₩ Diem.* *lbs.*	*oz.*	*drs.*
Oatmeal	7	0	2	8	Molasses for Gruel	7	0	0	8
Flour, 12 per cent., for Bread	6	1	3	8	Salt	7	0	0	12
Do. do.	1	1	2	0	Barley	4	0	0	8
Tea	7	0	0	3	Peas	1	0	1	0
Sugar	7	0	1	0	Vegetables	7	1	0	0
Meat, fresh	4	0	10	0	Soap	7	0	0	5
Do., salt	1	0	10	0	Tobacco	7	0	0	4
Bacon	1	0	6	0	Pepper	5	0	$\frac{1}{100}$	0
Suet	1	0	2	0					
Flour, 12 per cent., for Soup	5	0	0	8					
Do., for Pudding	1	0	8	0					

For Materials for Yeast see No. 19.

No. 1. Dietary.

Breakfast, Daily.— Gruel—1 Pint, made with 2½ oz. Oatmeal and ½ oz. Molasses.
Bread—8 oz.

Dinner — *On Mondays, Wednesdays, Fridays, and Saturdays.* — Fresh Meat—10 oz.: Beef and Mutton alternately.
Soup—1 Pint, made with 4 oz. mixed Vegetables, ½ oz. Flour, ½ oz. Barley, and 1-100th oz. Pepper.
Potatoes—12 oz.
Bread—6 oz.

Do. on Tuesdays — Bacon—6 oz.
Potatoes—8 oz.
Green Vegetables—8 oz., or an equivalent in Broad Beans or Peas.
Bread—6 oz.

Do. on Thursdays — Salt Meat—10 oz.
Soup—1 Pint, made with 4 oz mixed Vegetables, ½ oz. Flour, 1 oz. Peas, and 1-100 oz. Pepper.
Potatoes—12 oz.
Bread—6 oz.

Do. on Sundays — Potatoes—16 oz.
Bread—4 oz.
Pudding—16 oz., made with 2 oz. Suet, 8 oz. Flour, and 6 oz. Water.

Supper, Daily— Bread—12 oz.
Tea—1 Pint, made with 3-16th oz. Tea and 1 oz. Sugar.

nevertheless to obey instantly, but may complain afterwards if he shall think fit to the Commandant.

47. He is on all occasions, when passing a Civil or Military Officer to salute in a respectful manner by touching his cap.

48. He is at all times and in all places to conduct himself with the utmost order and regularity, and at every muster as well as in marching to and from labour he is to preserve the strictest silence.

49. He is not to have in his possession any article or thing whatever, either of food, clothing, or otherwise, except such as shall have been issued to him, or sanctioned by the Commandant, tobacco and all articles of luxury being especially prohibited.

50. He is on no account to absent himself from his gang, or appointed place of work, or when in barracks to leave the yard to which he belongs, or enter any other hut than his own, without express permission.

51. He is always to appear as clean in his person and dress as circumstances will admit he is to take care that his clothing, boots, bedding, plate, pannican, and spoon, are marked with his local number, and he is not to damage wilfully, give away, lend or exchange any of these articles, on any pretence whatever.

52. Should any article issued or entrusted to him be lost or damaged, he is to report the same immediately to his Overseer.

53. If in chains, he is held responsible that his irons are perfect, and not ovalled or too large.

54. He is not to perform any private work or labour whatever unless ordered to do so by his Overseer, or some superior authority.

55. He is not to send or receive any letters or packages, except through the Commandment, who will exercise his discretion in opening them and ascertaining their contents.

56. He is not to hold communication with any of the military, or with any sailor or person not belonging to the Settlement, except when on duty.

57. Should he connive at any breach of the laws or of the Settlement regulations, he will be considered as an accessary, and be liable to punishment accordingly.

No. 2. Ration.

FOR CONVICTS AT LIGHT LABOUR.

ARTICLES.	No. of Days Weekly.	Scale ₩ Diem.			ARTICLES.	No. of Days Weekly.	Scale ₩ Diem.		
		lbs.	oz.	drs.			lbs.	oz.	drs.
Oatmeal	7	0	2	0	Molasses for Gruel	7	0	0	8
Flour, 12 per cent., for Bread	6	1	2	0	Salt	7	0	0	12
Do. do.	1	1	0	8	Barley	4	0	0	8
Tea	7	0	0	3	Peas	1	0	1	0
Sugar	7	0	1	0	Vegetables	7	1	0	0
Meat, fresh	4	0	8	0	Soap	7	0	0	5
Do., salt	1	0	8	0	Tobacco	7	0	0	4
Bacon	1	0	4	0	Pepper	5	0	1/100	0
Suet	1	0	1	8					
Flour, 12 per cent., for Soup	5	0	0	8					
Do., for Pudding	1	0	6	0					

For Materials for Yeast see No. 19.

No. 2. Dietary.

Breakfast, Daily.—
- Gruel—1 Pint, made with 2 oz. Oatmeal and ½ oz. Molasses.
- Bread—6 oz.

Dinner On Mondays, Wednesdays, Fridays, and Saturdays.
- Fresh Meat—8 oz.: Beef and Mutton alternately.
- Soup—1 Pint, made with 4 oz. mixed Vegetables, ½ oz. Flour, ½ oz. Barley, and 1-100th oz. Pepper.
- Potatoes—12 oz.
- Bread—6 oz.

Do. on Tuesdays
- Bacon—4 oz.
- Potatoes—8 oz.
- Green Vegetables—8 oz., or an equivalent in Broad Beans or Peas.
- Bread—6 oz.

Do. on Thursdays
- Salt Meat—8 oz.
- Soup—1 Pint, made with 4 oz mixed Vegetables, ½ oz. Flour, 1 oz. Peas, and 1-100 oz. Pepper.
- Potatoes—12 oz.
- Bread 6 oz.

Do. on Sundays
- Potatoes—16 oz.
- Bread—4 oz.
- Pudding—12 oz., made with 1½ oz. Suet, 6 oz. Flour, and 4½ oz. Water.

Supper, Daily—
- Bread—12 oz.
- Tea—1 Pint, made with 3-16th oz. Tea and 1 oz. Sugar.

58. A Record Book is to be kept as heretofore of the conduct of every convict at the Settlement; a page will be allotted to each man, on one side of which will be entered every offence committed and the punishment awarded, and on the other side every instance of meritorious or praiseworthy conduct.

No. 7. Ration.

FOR PAUPERS AND INVALIDS—THE INDUSTRIOUS AND WELL-CONDUCTED.

Articles.	No. of Days Weekly.	Scale ⅌ Diem. lbs.	oz.	drs.	Articles.	No. of Days Weekly.	Scale ⅌ Diem. lbs.	oz.	drs.
Oatmeal	7	0	2	0	Salt	7	0	0	12
Flour	7	1	0	8	Barley	5	0	0	8
Tea	7	0	0	3	Vegetables	7	1	0	0
Sugar	7	0	1	0	Soap	7	0	0	5
Meat, fresh	2	0	8	0	Pepper	5	0	1/100	0
„ Heads, Necks, &c. equivalent to	3	0	6	0	Tobacco	7	0	0	4
Bacon	1	0	4	0					
Suet	1	0	1	8					
Flour, 12 per cent., for Soup	5	0	0	8					
Do., for Pudding	1	0	6	0					
Molasses	7	0	0	8					

For Materials for Yeast see No. 19.

No. 7. Dietary.

Breakfast, Daily.— Gruel—1 Pint, made with 2 oz. Oatmeal and ½ oz. Molasses.
Bread—6 oz.

Dinner On Mondays, Wednesdays, and Fridays. Meat—6 oz., including at the authorised equivalent in weight of Heads, Hocks, Necks, and Neat's Feet, and made into 1 Pint of Soup, with 4 oz. Vegetables, ½ oz. Barley, ½ oz. Flour, and 1-100th oz. Pepper.
Potatoes—12 oz.
Bread—4 oz.

Do. on Thursdays and Saturdays Fresh Meat—8 oz.
Soup—1 Pint, made with 4 oz. mixed Vegetables, ½ oz. Barley, ½ oz. Flour, & 1-100 oz. Pepper
Potatoes—12 oz.
Bread—4 oz.

Do. on Tuesdays. Bacon—4 oz.
Potatoes—8 oz.
Mixed Vegetables—8 oz., or an equivalent in Broad Beans or Peas.
Bread—4 oz.

Do. on Sundays

Supper, Daily. Tea—3-16th oz., Sugar 1 oz., made into 1 Pint of Tea.
Bread—12 oz.

59. Each man will be allowed

One Blanket
One Rug
One Bedtick

which will be replaced only when fairly worn out, or destroyed by unavoidable accident.

60. Clothing will be supplied to each man, every six months, as follows:

One Jacket
One Waistcoat
One pair of Trousers
One Shirt
One pair of Ancle Boots
One Cap.

61. There will be a regular evening school after the labours of the day are over at which the fundamental parts of education only are to be taught; as many convicts as can be accommodated will be permitted to attend, monitors having been chosen from the better informed.

No. 6. Ration.

PUNISHMENT IN CLOSE SOLITARY CONFINEMENT.

ARTICLES.	*No. of Days Weekly.*	*Scale ₩ Diem.* *lbs.*	*oz.*	*drs.*	ARTICLES.	*No. of Days Weekly.*	*Scale ₩ Diem.* *lbs.*	*oz.*	*drs.*
Flour, 12 per cent.		0	12	0	Soap		0	0	5
Salt for Bread.....................		0	0	8					

For Materials for Yeast see No. 19.

No. 6. Dietary.

Bread—1 lb. per diem.
Water—*ad lib.*

If close Solitary Confinement is continued above 7 days, Penal Class Diet to be given on the 8th day, and every 4th day afterwards.

Left: The penitentiary dining hall. Below: Views of Port Arthur when it was occupied by convicts.

Best-selling Recipe Books

from Southern Holdings Pty. Ltd.

The Australian Apple Recipe Book

Includes 148 top recipes, plus orchard photographs and calendar, apple varieties, and historical apples. 10th reprint.

The Australian Banana Recipe Book

Straight from tropical Queensland comes this extensive range of fabulous banana recipes - now this universal health food can be fully explored. Includes banana details and pictures.

The Australian Convict Recipe Book

Includes 150 practical recipes plus historical photographs, convict rules and rations and the unabridged story of Bessie Baldwin.

The Australian Historical Recipe Book

Join John Caire in exploring Australia's most popular recipes over the years, including some introduced from Europe and Asia. Includes historical photographs and the story 'Living Off The Land'. Features Bush & Spade recipes, Steamboat cooking, and Homestead recipes, as well as John's own restaurant recipes.

The Australian Huon Valley Recipe Book

Authentic country recipes from the fine food centre of Tasmania. Selected from treasured family recipe collections. Beautiful Huon scenes and the settlement story are included.

The Australian National Trust Recipe Book

A balanced collection of the most popular tried and true family recipes; this is a book to treasure over the years to come.

The Australian Potato Surprise Recipe Book

155 top Potato recipes for all occasions: the versatility of this universal food is fully exploited - a must for every kitchen.

The Great Australian Bite Recipe Book

An exciting approach to Barbecues by a top chef. Marinades, butters, breads, kebabs and barbecues galore combine to make this a 'must have' recipe book!

The Great Australian Pumpkin Recipe Book

Includes 110 pumpkin recipes (including ice cream), plus the Great Pumpkin story and Growing & Caring for Pumpkins.

Recipe Books per copy: .$9.95 (GST Inc.) plus $3.30 postage and packing

(Fundraisers, please enquire about our special offer)

ORDER by EMAIL from
geejtee@bigpond.com or Phone (03) 6247 9337